The Library of Explorers and Exploration

AMERIGO VESPUCCI

Italian Explorer of the Americas

Kurt Ray

the rosen publishing group's
rosen
central

Published in 2004 by The Rosen Publishing Group, Inc.
29 East 21st Street, New York, NY 10010

Library of Congress Cataloging-in-Publication Data

Ray, Kurt.
Amerigo Vespucci : Italian explorer of the Americas / Kurt Ray.— 1st ed.
   p. cm. — (The Library of explorers and exploration)
Summary: A biography of the Italian-born explorer who was the first
person to realize North America was a separate continent.
Includes bibliographical references and index.
ISBN 0-8239-3615-5 (lib. bdg.)
1. Vespucci, Amerigo, 1451–1512—Juvenile literature.
2. Explorers—America—Biography—Juvenile literature.
3. Explorers—Spain—Biography—Juvenile literature.
4. Explorers—Portugal—Biography—Juvenile literature.
5. America—Discovery and exploration—Spanish—Juvenile literature.
6. America—Discovery and exploration—Portuguese—Juvenile literature.
[1. Vespucci, Amerigo, 1451–1512. 2. Explorers. 3. America—
Discovery and exploration—Spanish. 4. America—Discovery and
exploration—Portuguese.]
I. Title. II. Series.
E125.V5 R29 2002
970.01'6'092—dc21
                           2002003359

Manufactured in the United States of America

CONTENTS

Introduction: Understanding
   the New World   5
1. Ancient Questions   8
2. A Florentine Family   23
3. The Mystery of the Letters   41
4. A Voyage for Spain   53
5. A Voyage for Portugal   68
6. Return to Fame   88
   Chronology   100
   Glossary   102
   For More Information   106
   For Further Reading   108
   Bibliography   109
   Index   110

Though Amerigo Vespucci was never elevated to the status of his colleague Christopher Columbus, his talents were appreciated by many. Residents of Florence inscribed a passage on the Vespucci family mansion, describing Amerigo as "a noble Florentine, who by the discovery of America rendered his own and his country's name illustrious; the Amplifier of the World."

INTRODUCTION

UNDERSTANDING THE NEW WORLD

Rationally, let it be said in a whisper, experience is certainly worth more than theory.
—Letter from Amerigo Vespucci to Lorenzo di Pier Francesco de' Medici, 1499

Amerigo Vespucci was not the first European to set foot in the New World. The Viking Leif Eriksson led an expedition to North America around AD 1000, but the Norse discovery went unrecognized for many centuries. It was nearly 500 years later that another European explorer sailed across the Atlantic Ocean. That explorer was Christopher Columbus, who first set foot in the New World in 1492. Columbus was certain that the islands he found were located just off the coast of Asia, and he named them "the Indies." In fact, he was in the Caribbean Sea situated between North and South America.

Vespucci arrived in the New World soon after Columbus did, but his experience was quite different. Vespucci's breakthrough was to understand that he was not in Asia. By remaining open to all possibilities, Vespucci was able to understand that the Indies were part of a new world that was nowhere near Asia. The world was actually much larger than Columbus had believed. There were still entire continents to discover. These ideas frightened Columbus, who, obsessed with his "discovery," desperately wanted to remain true to his false beliefs. Vespucci was far more concerned with reality.

Born during the Renaissance, Vespucci was a skilled man of superior intellect. Fluent in several languages as well as an excellent mathematician and mapmaker, Vespucci used everything he knew to solve the mysteries of the New World. He focused only on facts available to him and not theory. If those facts changed during the course of his explorations, he adjusted his opinions and continued searching for answers. This was a new method of understanding the world—a newfound enlightenment after many years of seeking guidance about geography from only religious sources. Vespucci's open mind helped him chart unfamiliar coastlines, deal responsibly with his crew, and even live peacefully with cannibals.

Vespucci's legacy is as fascinating as it is puzzling. Most of what is known about his life may be found from a series of mysterious letters, some of which historians doubt were written by him at all. Some reflect his patience and attention to detail, while others seem only to exaggerate his stories. Still others appear to be completely invented, like those that take credit for Columbus's discoveries and other navigators' journeys.

These letters made many people angry long after Vespucci had died, especially because both North and South America were named after him, an honor that many felt he didn't deserve because Columbus had set foot in the New World before him. Still, it's important to understand Vespucci's groundbreaking work: He advanced the study of navigation, cartography, and astronomy. He made careful observations of foreign cultures without dismissing traditions that disgusted him. Vespucci chose not to pass judgment on the New World. Confident and curious, Vespucci utilized his skills to expand the world's knowledge, encouraging Americans to be proud to live in a country that bears his name.

1

ANCIENT QUESTIONS

It was my intention to see whether I could round a cape of land which Ptolemy calls the Cape of Cattigara.
—Letter from Vespucci to Lorenzo di Pier
Francesco de' Medici, July 18, 1500

Even though Amerigo Vespucci was a remarkable mapmaker, mathematician, navigator, and author, his work relied on the discoveries of men who lived hundreds of years before he was born. Even the tools he used were primitive and untrustworthy. These instruments, which included the astrolabe to measure latitude (distances north and south), and the quadrant to calculate the altitude of celestial bodies from the horizon, were the same tools used by ancient scientists centuries earlier. Incredibly, these men managed to learn much about the world without the aid of today's modern equipment. Their discoveries would assist Vespucci in his own groundbreaking work nearly 1,500 years later.

Vespucci's methods for calculating longitude proved far more accurate than traditional means of dead reckoning. In fact, the skills of reading the locations of the moon and other celestial bodies against charts he brought with him helped Vespucci estimate the size of Earth's surface quite accurately—he was just fifty miles short of its actual circumference.

Ptolemy's Wisdom

Ancient scientists were perplexed by absorbing questions, such as the exact size of the earth, both before and during Vespucci's life. They also pondered how much of Earth's surface was covered with land and how much was covered with water. As scientists, they had few ways of sharing ideas between cities and countries, making the collection of any data nearly impossible. Yet, some of the brightest scientists in history still had the ability to dissect the most difficult questions of all time. One of these great thinkers was Claudius Ptolemy.

Ptolemy was born and lived in Alexandria, Egypt, though he was probably from a Greek family. We know that he died between AD 161 and 180, but we know little else about his life as few records about that period in history remain. He was most likely a student of Theon, an Egyptian mathematician who made observations of the cycles of the sun and the moon. Ptolemy referenced the work of Theon, as well as many other prominent thinkers of his time, when he wrote his most famous work, *Almagest*.

Almagest was a gigantic project, including thirteen volumes that discussed Ptolemy's understanding of the stars and planets, including their positions and brightness. Though much of *Almagest* later proved inaccurate, it is remarkable how much Ptolemy really did understand about the solar system. Using mathematical principles to guide him, Ptolemy theorized that the earth was round and that the other planets and stars revolved around it. While we know now that the earth does not stand still in space, Ptolemy's theories were revolutionary. He was able to map out the positions of the planets in relation to each other, showing that some were closer to the earth and others were farther away.

Ptolemy used similar methods when he wrote another groundbreaking work called *Geography*. Combining his knowledge of the world, mathematical principles, and the stories of places visited by ancient explorers, Ptolemy created a map of the world. His map included only the lands that were known to him at the time: Africa, most of Asia, and Europe.

On Ptolemy's world map, the earth was divided into top and bottom halves, now called hemispheres. The line he used for this division became known as the equator. Ptolemy's map was curved, using lines of measurement that ran north and south to chart different positions on the earth

The image on the next two pages shows one of Ptolemy's maps of the world, which he drew in about AD 150. It was based on his assumption that Earth was flat, and showed only the world that was known at the time, Europe and northern Asia. Ptolemy, or Claudius Ptolemaeus, is considered by many to be the father of modern geography. He developed the system of grids and he coined the vocabulary of "width," or latitude, and "length," or longitude. This map of the world was one of many that originated in his famous work *Geography*.

(Vespucci later helped to develop this idea further and may have been one of the first persons to call the measurements longitude, part of a system that is still in use today). Though *Geography* was primitive, the outlines of the continents drawn by Ptolemy are surprisingly accurate and look familiar when compared against modern maps.

After the fall of the Roman Empire (around AD 500), Ptolemy's work was largely forgotten, along with the works of many other scientists, explorers, and artists. It was revived later by Arab scholars who made translations and handwritten copies of *Almagest* and *Geography*. Explorers used these handwritten copies of Ptolemy's works throughout the Far East and in the Islamic empires from AD 700 through the Middle Ages.

The Dark Ages

During the years AD 462–800 very little European history was recorded. This approximated time period is known as the Dark Ages. The Roman Empire (509 BC–AD 500) had connected and unified many different parts of the world, allowing a relationship between those parts, as well as a sharing of information that was once isolated. During the Dark Ages, individual sections of the old empire became divided sections with fluctuating boundaries, and often fought with each other for increased power.

At this time, science, literature, and the arts were not shared widely, and public education was rare. Though art was still being created, it was created for the glory of God, and artists remained anonymous. Rather than encouraging education, communities relied upon people for manual labor such as farming.

The Dark Ages saw a dramatic increase in the influence of Christianity (in Europe) and Islam (in the Middle East), and religious devotion was considered a sign of virtue. The Roman Catholic Church was very wealthy, which also contributed to its power. As the Church became deeply involved with the monarchy of many European countries, popes often appointed leaders of kingdoms, making their relationship political instead of just moral. Unfortunately, this also increased the corruption of leadership. Over time, people grew worried that the Church was more concerned with amassing money and property than with guiding people and their moral standards.

Beginning in AD 1096, the Church exerted its power in a military campaign known as the Crusades. These battles were a violent effort to expand the extent and influence of Christianity. They were also an effort to spread European culture to the east into Asian countries. Convinced that their culture and beliefs were superior to those of other countries, Europeans used force to conquer foreign peoples.

But Europeans were not the only people to employ violence to spread their faith. Islamic crusaders often fought Christians with the same aims in mind. These conflicts set the stage for the discovery of new lands over the next several centuries and a struggle to establish superiority. At the same time it exposed both sides to the science and arts of the other. In fact, the only copies of ancient Greek and Roman texts initially available in Europe were from Arabic translations, most of the originals having been lost much earlier.

The Rebirth of Knowledge

By AD 1300, ideas began to change. Education was again encouraged and Europeans were rediscovering the important scientific work that had been done many centuries earlier, such as Ptolemy's writings. Though Ptolemy's original hand-drawn maps had been lost, the *Geography* still existed in Arabic, and Western European scholars were able to re-create the world map based on his measurements.

Knowledge and learning fueled the next several centuries of discovery, a time that is known as the Renaissance, or rebirth. During the Renaissance, the philosophy of "humanism," which focused on the importance of individual thought and discovery, became popular. Humanist educators based their teachings on the works of ancient Greek and Roman writers and artists, which were considered superior examples of culture

The Crusades were military expeditions that were inspired by religious beliefs to spread Christianity and regain Palestine from the Muslims. The word "crusade" originates from *crux*, the Latin word for "cross." A red-colored cross, like the one shown in this illustration, was commonly sewn to soldiers' garments and flags.

and thought. Though centered in Italian city-states such as Florence, Genoa, and Venice, the Renaissance soon spread to other European countries, too, including both France and Germany.

The Renaissance also laid claim to important developments such as modern printing. During the 1440s, a German named Johannes Gutenberg invented the first printing press, an invention that forever changed the way in which knowledge was shared. At last, a book could be machine-printed instead of copied by hand. With the renewed desire for education, the printing press allowed literate people the opportunity to learn about any subject they desired. As a result, the demand for knowledge increased at a very rapid pace.

Tales of Adventure

During the Renaissance, stories of exploration and adventure were extremely popular. The public demanded to learn about explorers like Marco Polo and Christopher Columbus, who had both been sent abroad by European rulers to find new trade routes, gold, and spices.

Europeans were especially intrigued by Marco Polo's tales of exploration. Born in Venice, Italy, to a family of jewel traders, Polo joined his father and his uncle on a journey to Asia during the late 1200s. The Polos lived in China, known then as Cathay, for seventeen years, as the

This richly illustrated manuscript page dates from 1455 and is part of the *Mazarin Bible*, one of the first printed books in European history. This book, along with the *Thirty-Six Line Bible* and other books of the period, was known as *incunabula*, from the Latin word for cradle. These books were generally large quarto (one sheet folded to make eight pages) size, bound in calfskin over boards of wood, decorated with red initials and ornamental borders, and carried no title page.

guests of the Mongol ruler Kublai Khan. Marco Polo served as a diplomat for the Khan, traveling all over China. Periodically, Polo returned to the Khan's court to tell him stories of the places he had visited.

After many years in China, the Khan permitted the Polos to return home to Italy. They were welcomed as heroes in the city of Venice, and Marco Polo was made an honorary commander of the Venetian navy. He joined forces with a writer, Rustichello, who wrote *Description of the World* (later known as the *Travels of Marco Polo*), a best-selling French translation of Polo's stories that was widely published. Polo died in 1324, but the invention of the printing press kept his stories very much alive.

Polo's detailed description of his travels excited many Europeans. Through his tales, they learned about Asian customs, beautiful architecture and clothing, and even the geography of the countries Polo had visited. Though Rustichello probably exaggerated the details of the adventures to make them more romantic, there is little doubt that Polo's stories influenced many other explorers, including Columbus, whose copy of *The Travels of Marco Polo* still exists. Columbus pored over Polo's geographic descriptions when he went in search of China and India and was known to have made many notes in the margins of his edition.

Mongol emperor Kublai Khan is shown giving his golden seal to the Polos at his new capital Cambaluc (Beijing) in this illustration from *Le Livre des Merveilles du Monde* (The Book of the Wonders of the World) by Jean de Mandeville. Marco Polo described the famous palace and its adornments of "dragons, beasts and birds, knights and gods, and other subjects."

Different Worlds, Different Viewpoints

Columbus was certainly driven to find a western ocean route to Asia. Sailing on behalf of Spain, Columbus's expeditions went in search of gold, silver, and spices. Columbus was also a deeply religious man, a devout Catholic who attended mass regularly. He believed that God had a special destiny in mind for him, which was to convert native peoples to Christianity.

While searching for Asia, Columbus discovered a new world instead, but he stubbornly refused to believe that the lands he found were anything but the Orient. Thinking he had discovered islands off the coast of India, he named the inhabitants "Indians," a name that has remained for centuries. Columbus was fooled into thinking he had reached Asia because he was unwilling to believe that the earth might be larger than previously thought.

Though Vespucci and Columbus were friends and supporters of each other's work, Vespucci's mind was more open to new possibilities. This independent thinking led to his greater understanding of the world and its geography. Aided by Ptolemy's *Geography*, Vespucci was willing to make educated guesses about the earth's size and prove those theories true.

2

A FLORENTINE FAMILY

However, let me not pass over in silence the more obvious pleasures: to devote oneself to reading and writing . . . to read what our forerunners have written and to write what later generations may wish to read.
—Francis Petrarch, *The Life of Solitude,* 1346

Amerigo Vespucci was born during the height of the Renaissance and was the third of four sons born to his mother, Lisabetta. Although most documents consider his exact date of birth to be March 9, 1451, many other historians and scholars claim he was born on that same day and month, but three years later, in 1454. In either case, the spirit of the arts and of learning was well under way in Florence, Italy, Vespucci's birth city, as well as the rest of Europe. Florence, like many Italian provinces, was experiencing a rebirth of culture and science. Florentines were enjoying art and music, and questioning the laws of the physical world around them.

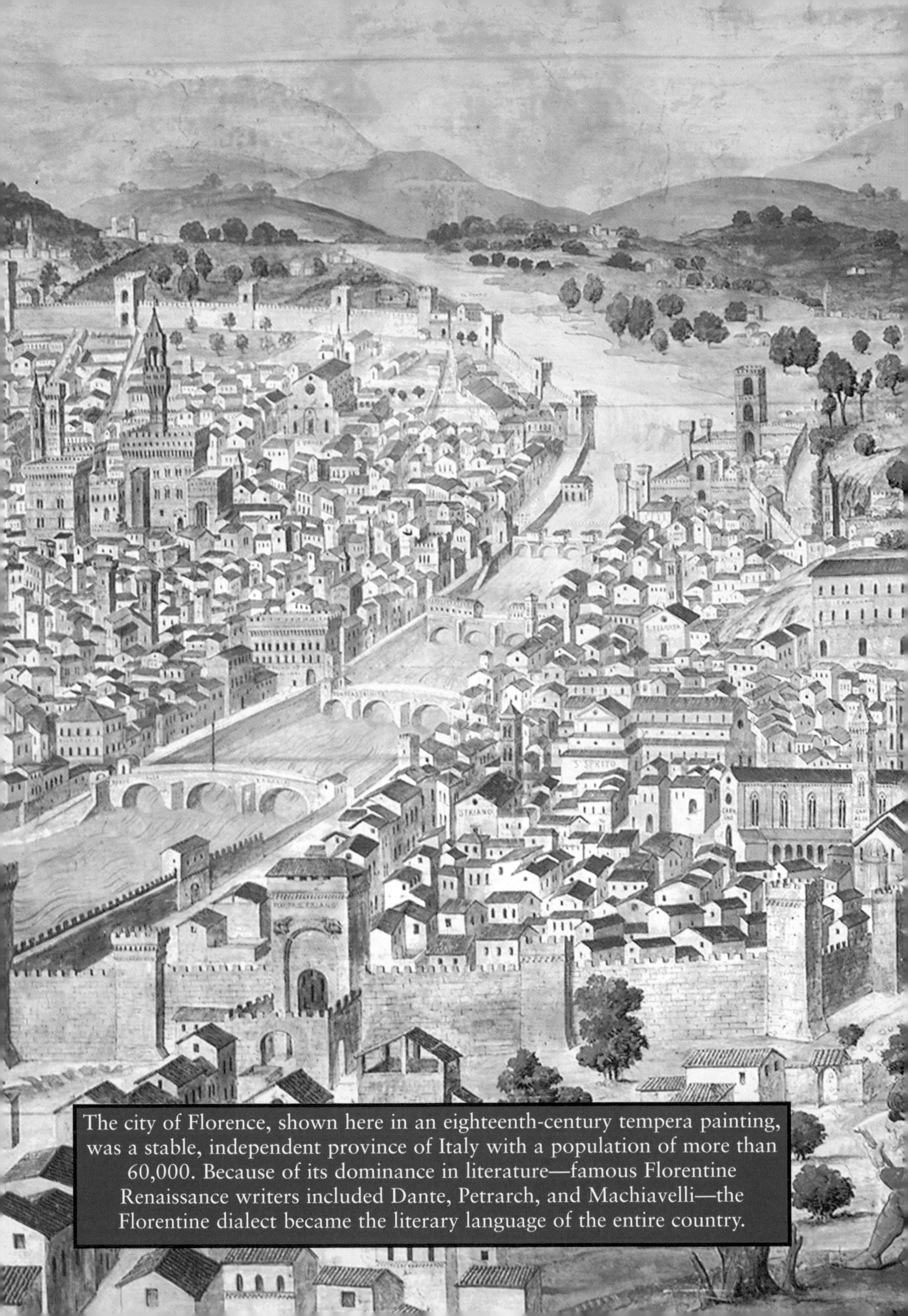

The city of Florence, shown here in an eighteenth-century tempera painting, was a stable, independent province of Italy with a population of more than 60,000. Because of its dominance in literature—famous Florentine Renaissance writers included Dante, Petrarch, and Machiavelli—the Florentine dialect became the literary language of the entire country.

The Vespucci family was neither poor nor wealthy, but they were well-respected members of the Florentine community. Vespucci's father, Nastagio, and grandfather, Amerigo, both served as secretaries of the Senate, a political body that ruled Florence, and were well acquainted with the influential Florentine family the de' Medicis.

Though Florence was not ruled by a king, the Medici family had enormous power and influence during Vespucci's lifetime because they were successful bankers who had business connections throughout Europe. Their money bought them political power, but they were passionate humanists as well, supporting the arts and encouraging individual education for the Florentine people. The Medici family often acted as patrons of the arts as well, and at various times assisted artists including Michelangelo Buonarroti, Leonardo da Vinci, and Sandro Botticelli. One of Vespucci's uncles, Guidoantonio, was also employed by the Medici family as their ambassador to France.

Squares and Towers

Florence was a major center for the manufacturing of woolen cloth, in addition to supporting hundreds of other skilled artisans. Many of these artists were associated with *arti*, or guilds, associations that helped set standards of craftsmanship and worked to protect

25

the interests of artisans. The creation of guilds was extremely progressive at the time, but not unusual in the thriving political culture of Florence. Guild members were mainly wealthy Florentines who were influential in Italian society and politics.

Florence, situated along the banks of the Arno River about 100 miles inland from the shores of the Mediterranean Sea, was a thriving banking center, unlike Italy's port cities such as Genoa or Venice, which were famous for their trading power. Florence's narrow streets were lined with crowded tenements and massive stone walls, but behind many of those barriers lay beautiful formal courtyards. Beyond the populated city, which during Vespucci's lifetime rivaled that of London, lay a graceful countryside.

As a youth, Vespucci was an occasional daydreamer who watched boats come and go along the Arno River, just blocks from his family's two-story townhouse in the Ognissanti section of Florence.

Breathtaking works of art, such as Donatello's sculpture of David, the first nude crafted in the classical style since antiquity, and architecture that included fortresslike palaces, were being created during Vespucci's youth. He would have also

Alessandro di Mariano Filipepi, known as Sandro Botticelli (1445–1510), was a friend of the Medici family, lived in their palace, and painted many works in Florence during Vespucci's lifetime. This illustration, a detail of the painting *Primavera* ("Spring Season"), still hangs in Florence's Uffizi Gallery.

In the Middle Ages, nutmeg was thought to have magical powers, but it was more commonly used to disguise the foul flavor of rotting meats.

been familiar with the Pitti Palace, an estate belonging to the Medici family, which contained paintings by Raphael and Titian. Directly behind the palace were the Boboli Gardens, with its elegant grounds, sparkling fountains, and immaculately groomed hedges. The Piazza San Lorenzo was home to a beautiful church and an enormous library, which later included a stairway that was designed by Michelangelo. Even the central market of Florence was breathtaking, teeming with colorful woolen and silk fabrics and the aroma of spices from around the world.

Italy was considered an important center of European trade because of its proximity to both the Middle East and Asia. Using the frequently traveled seas, merchants imported luxury items like silks and tapestries from India, and valuable spices like cloves and nutmeg from present-day Indonesia. Asia was also the source for diamonds, rubies, and pearls.

Obtaining such beautiful materials was difficult, however. Traveling by land required long journeys through dangerous deserts, often by caravan. Turkish warriors, who frequently prevented European traders from crossing through their territory, made these journeys even more perilous. Traveling south and east by sea was a risky venture, too, and required careful navigation. Waters were stormy near the area later known as Africa's Cape of Good Hope, and many European ships were lost during Asian expeditions. These conditions increased the demand for a safer ocean route to Asia.

A Renaissance Education

Vespucci's two older brothers, Girolamo and Marco, were sent to the University of Pisa for a traditional scholastic education, one of the two prominent styles of teaching in Europe at the time. The scholastic style focused on logic and theology while the humanist style of education focused on grammar, history, poetry, and social responsibility. Vespucci was sent to his uncle Giorgio for this arts-based education, which was less traditional. Normally, a scholastic education prepared a student for a career in medicine, law, or religion, but Vespucci's father decided that his youngest son, Amerigo, should be taught differently.

Giorgio Vespucci was a priest, but his teachings were more in this humanist style, which opposed training someone to become only a doctor or craftsman. Instead, humanist educators, inspired by ancient Greek and Roman values, hoped to provide a broader, well-rounded education that allowed a student to be taught many things, including arts, athleticism, and science. This is the origin of the term "Renaissance Man," which is used to describe well-rounded individuals.

Vespucci's uncle taught him mathematics and ancient Greek philosophy. As a student, Vespucci read the works of great world authors, including the poetry of Petrarch, an author considered to be the first humanist. Vespucci practiced Latin, writing short notes to his father in the ancient language. He also became proficient in other languages, including Spanish and French. Vespucci was especially interested in learning about the world and he was an avid student of cosmography, which included both geography and astronomy. Because of this interest, his uncle introduced him to Ptolemy's *Geography*.

In fact, Vespucci's father may have hoped that Giorgio was providing his son with a humanistic education, since it seems likely that he had hoped Amerigo would follow in his footsteps as a political administrator. Vespucci did just that for a while, but it was soon apparent that he was better able to use his skills as a mapmaker and mathematician.

Expanding Horizons

In his early twenties, Vespucci went to work in Paris with his uncle Guidoantonio, who was the Medici ambassador to France. Vespucci worked as his uncle's secretary for several years and was put in charge of all business correspondence. The experience was valuable since he had access to his uncle's wealthy, well-educated associates. Vespucci was exposed to a different culture and was beginning to earn the trust of the powerful Medici family.

His experiences in business helped him learn the power of diplomacy. From his uncle, Vespucci learned how to defuse tense situations by speaking carefully and considering all points of view. This skill became even more valuable years later when he encountered completely unfamiliar cultures in the New World.

In April 1482, when Vespucci was in his early thirties, his father died. Since Vespucci had been more successful than his brothers, he was now the main source of income for his family. In 1483, the Medicis invited Vespucci to manage the financial affairs of two of their youngest members, Lorenzo and Giovanni di Pier Francesco. Although his new clients were considerably younger than he was, Vespucci befriended them and was able to increase their profits through successful business dealings.

Lorenzo di Pier Francesco de' Medici *(second from left)*, known to the Florentines as "Lorenzo the Magnificent," ruled Florence with his younger brother Giulino from 1469 to 1478. He is best remembered for his support of literature and the arts.

Managing the finances of the di Pier Francesco brothers gave Vespucci reason to travel a great deal. Though he was based in Florence, Vespucci took business trips to neighboring Italian cities such as Genoa and Rome. He also traveled to Spain. Spain, particularly the city of Seville, enchanted Vespucci, which reminded him of his home city. Like Florence, Seville was located along the banks of a river, the Guadalquivir, and was flourishing with art and new ideas. Seville was also a similar city in that it welcomed people of many different cultures. In 1492, Vespucci moved to Seville permanently. Later he would be named a Spanish citizen.

While in Spain, Vespucci was assigned to manage a new bank branch for the Medici family. He reported to a man named Giannotto Berardi, a businessman who formed a partnership with Columbus in order to provide financing for his upcoming expedition. In August 1492, Columbus's first expedition set sail across the Atlantic Ocean.

During Vespucci's youth, most people knew that the world was round. Navigators like Columbus (who was also an Italian, born in 1451) hoped that a safer water route to Asia could be found by sailing west from Europe across the Atlantic Ocean.

The "Indies," the territory that Columbus claimed to have discovered in 1492, were actually islands in the Caribbean Sea, south of what is now the United States. Columbus thought he had reached Asian territories on the eastern side of the Indus River, which runs through present-day China and Pakistan.

Columbus was aware of the existence of Japan, but he believed that it was only about 3,000 miles west of Spain's Canary Islands. In fact, the distance is nearly 12,000 miles. Columbus had grossly underestimated the circumference of the earth.

Despite his mistakes, Columbus had good reason to believe his thinking was correct. Ptolemy's *Geography* supported this worldview. In addition, the famous Italian mathematician Paolo Toscanelli also believed that Asia could be reached by sailing west. We know that Columbus and Toscanelli corresponded with each other and supported each other's ideas. Toscanelli was associated with the same monastery as Vespucci's uncle Giorgio. It is even possible that Vespucci studied with him.

Merchants and seamen gather along the Guadalquivir River in the port of Seville, Spain, in this detail of a sixteenth-century painting by Alonso Sanchez Coello. Vespucci, quite taken with the city upon his first visit there in 1483, was probably very impressed with the sights of its bell tower, Giralda, and the Cathedral of Seville, one of the largest in the world.

The Lure of Discovery

When Columbus returned to Spain in 1493, he was hailed as a hero. Despite the strange people he had seen on his voyage—indigenous natives he called Indians, but who others felt looked distinctively non-Asian—Columbus announced that he had successfully traveled to the Indies. Columbus's return was also met with disappointment. He returned with very little gold or silver, not the spoils of treasures of which he had once imagined. Still, his discoveries were astonishing. Not surprisingly, Spain and Portugal began to argue about rights to any new territories he had explored.

Columbus began making plans for a second voyage almost immediately. As he discussed his plans, he bragged about his knowledge of geography, and he said in a letter to King Ferdinand and Queen Isabella, "I see that the world is not so large as the common crowd say it is. I am not one of those carried astray by the new calculations. This is a fact, and whatever any one says to the contrary is only words." Columbus had proven himself a great sailor, but he refused to give any thought to the possibility that he had not reached Asia.

Isabella became queen of Castile in 1474 on the death of her brother. She married Ferdinand of Aragon in 1469. Both are shown with Columbus in this nineteenth-century French painting. Legend has it that Isabella so believed in Columbus's Enterprise of the Indies that she offered to pawn her own jewelry to support his sea venture across the Atlantic Ocean in 1492.

Other scientists, however, were not so sure of his "discoveries." Through his association with Columbus's financial supporter Berardi, Vespucci had access to the details of Columbus's travels. Because Vespucci had been a collector of maps all his life, he knew how to calculate both latitude (distances north and south), and the more recently developed longitude (distances east and west). Vespucci had serious questions about the nature of what Columbus had discovered. He wanted to find a way to answer those questions.

Columbus Tries Again

Berardi and Vespucci helped finance a second voyage for Columbus. It left Spain in September 1493. The voyage marked the beginning of a downturn in Columbus's reputation. During his first expedition, when he sailed to Hispaniola (later Haiti and the Dominican Republic), he had left behind thirty-nine sailors to build a fort. Sadly, the settlement had been burned and all the men killed by fierce natives, most likely the Carib Indians who were known for their aggression. In an attempt to keep his crew from turning on him, Columbus immediately sailed to a neighboring island and founded a newer settlement. He named it La Isabela.

This map of the Caribbean shows Florida, Cuba, and Hispaniola, which Columbus visited on his first and second voyages. Columbus was so uncertain that he would return safely to Spain that he wrote a brief account of his voyage, placed it in a bottle, and threw it overboard. He hoped that if his ship went down, at least the news of his discoveries might be known.

TERRE DE LA FLORIDE

PARTIE DE LA MER OCEANNE

LA COUBE

ESPAIGNOL

Jamaique

PARTIE DE LA MER DE LENTILLE

The natives on the island called their land Cuba, and Columbus interpreted this as a form of Kublai, as in Kublai Khan, the Mongol ruler that Marco Polo had described. Despite knowing that Cuba was an island, Columbus later insisted that it was part of a mainland. He convinced himself that Cuba was a remote corner of Asia and stubbornly refused to hear any other possible explanation for the rest of his life.

Vespucci, as well as other well-educated men, knew that the positions of Hispaniola and La Isabela did not agree with the stories of Marco Polo, or even Ptolemy's *Geography*. Though he did not yet suspect a new continent, Vespucci was puzzled by the facts of Columbus's journeys. Columbus did return from his second voyage with a small amount of gold, but he had still failed to encounter any natives who resembled people from Asian or Indian cultures.

King Ferdinand of Spain began granting permission for other explorers to search for a western route to Asia, fueling the fire that was already present in Vespucci's heart. Despite the fact that he was in his mid-forties at this point, Vespucci, at the encouragement of the Spanish monarchy, decided to explore the New World himself.

3

THE MYSTERY
OF THE LETTERS

The first voyage appears, both from internal and external evidence, to be imaginary.
—Excerpt from an 1894 publication of Vespucci's letters by the Hakluyt Society

Centuries after Vespucci's death, historians are still debating the exact details of his travels. Despite the existence of several letters that were apparently written in his handwriting, there remain claims that the missives are fictional. Though Vespucci had nothing to do with naming the continents that bear his name, there are those who still feel that the Americas should have been called the Columbias, in honor of Christopher Columbus.

Although his expeditions led to the slave trade and brought conquest and disease to Native Americans, Christopher Columbus is remembered for his remarkable journeys of discovery in the New World. He is respected for founding one of the first established colonies in the Americas. However, he truly believed that the New World he had set foot in was actually Asia.

The Problem of the Letters

Much of what we know about Vespucci's life is drawn from letters he wrote to friends and business associates. Though many of the letters are personal in nature, they were probably written for an audience of several people, rather than just one recipient. Some of them were written in multiple copies, as though many people were meant to receive them. To further complicate matters, Vespucci was an excellent storyteller. Still, experts over the years have longed to understand the details that he left out.

One of the most puzzling mysteries of Vespucci's letters is the lack of names within them. Vespucci rarely refers to his crew members or expedition leaders. That information has since been learned from other sources, such as shipping records or captain's logs, but some historians believe that Vespucci deliberately left these names out so that he could make false claims. By not naming the men who traveled with him, it would be more difficult for other people to dispute what he said. The lack of names alone, though, is not enough to brand the letters as fakes.

In the case of Vespucci's letters to his former employer, Lorenzo di Pier Francesco de' Medici, it is possible that Medici already knew the names of the other people involved. In that case, Vespucci wouldn't need to identify the other members of his expeditions. It is also likely that there were some letters to Medici that have never been found—letters that might fill in the gaps left in the others that have survived.

Adding to the confusion of understanding the true meaning of Vespucci's letters is another problem related to their translation. It was not uncommon during his lifetime for any of his letters—or letters written by other well-known figures—to be translated into Latin and then distributed widely throughout Europe. The invention of the printing press during the fifteenth century made it possible for a larger audience to read about new places and ideas, and it is likely that Vespucci's letters were translated many times from their original source documents.

However, without seeing the original handwritten letters, it is impossible to know how accurate the translations were. Letters translated for public use were often altered. An unskilled translator might accidentally misinterpret the writer's intentions or even his or her writing style. Translations also made it easier for dishonest publishers to produce fake letters. Without a systemized mail service or other way of communicating information quickly, it was unlikely that the person whose name was being used would ever find out.

Letters to Lorenzo

The letters Vespucci wrote to Lorenzo di Pier Francesco de' Medici are known as the familiar letters. They are handwritten in Italian, and Lorenzo may have shared them with other family members and friends. For many years, their existence was forgotten until they were recovered during the eighteenth century. When they were finally published, experts debated whether they were actually written by Vespucci or someone else.

The familiar letters are fascinating pieces of history that carefully detail journeys that Vespucci took in 1499 and 1501. They include star charts, geographic notes, and interesting passages about the customs of the native peoples Vespucci encountered. In them, he considers revisions to Ptolemy's world map. The letters are so interesting that it's easy to understand why the public was excited to read them.

The image on the next two pages shows Vespucci charting stellar activity with an astrolabe. Although Vespucci explored more than 6,000 miles of South American coastline, he was better known as a nautical scientist than an explorer. The astrolabe, an instrument dating back more than 2,000 years, was used by sailors to aid them in navigating the sea. The astrolabe measures the positions of the stars and planets and is believed to have been invented by Hipparchus of Bithynia, a Greek scientist.

DANTHES
Aligerius
Florentinus
Poëta, Anno
Sal. M.CCC.
descripsit
IIII. stellas
Antarcticas
cap.˚ pr.˚ purg.

ALIGERIVS DANTHES

His verbis
ab Americo
Vespuccio
in suis
Epistolis
adductis.

Io mi volsi a man destra, e posimente
A l'altro polo, e vidi quattro stelle
Non viste mai fuer ch'a la prima gente,
Goder pareua il ciel di lor fiammelle;
O Settentrional vedruo sito,
Poi che priuato sei di mirar quelle.

Ego inde versus intuebar æthera,
Poli Nothi adnotaui ibi astra quattuor,
Nisi à priore gente, visa nemini.
Nitet, micatꝗ flamma quadrupla æthere,
Mihi plaga orbis orba nosse cerneris
Nequit videre quando tanta lumina.

Ioan. Stradanus inuent.   Ioan. Collaert sculp.

Mundus Novus

One of the most famous documents associated with Vespucci exists only in a Latin translation. Known as *Mundus Novus*, or "The New World," this document was first published in 1502 or 1503 in Italy. Though Vespucci was still alive at the time, we have no way of knowing if he actually wrote *Mundus Novus* or even if he knew of its publication.

Mundus Novus was supposedly a translation of a letter from Vespucci to Lorenzo de Pier Francesco de' Medici. And though it does resemble some of the letters to Medici, its tone and style are different enough to suggest a forgery. Still, the public believed that Vespucci had written *Mundus Novus,* and it had great success wherever it was published.

The basic details of the journey described in the *Mundus Novus* match the letters to Medici describing his voyage of 1501. However, its details are far more expressive, suggesting that a publisher wanted to exaggerate its facts, creating more of an adventure story out of what may have begun as merely a letter to a friend.

The *Letter to a Magnificent Lord*

Another letter published at about the same time was the *Lettera*, also known as the *Letter to a Magnificent Lord*, or *Four*

Voyages. It was supposedly a translation of a letter that Vespucci wrote to Piero Soderini, the head of Florence after the death of Lorenzo di Pier Francesco de' Medici. Soderini had a great interest in stories of exploration, and he had been a student of Vespucci's uncle Giorgio.

Even more than *Mundus Novus*, the *Lettera* is dramatic reading material. First published in 1505, the *Lettera* describes not two, but four separate voyages taken by Vespucci. Again, many of its details match the journeys described in the familiar letters. As in *Mundus Novus*, the details are exaggerated and more shocking than in the familiar letters, particularly when describing the behavior of native people. Most controversial is the suggestion that Vespucci first took a journey for Spain in 1497. In the *Lettera*, it is Vespucci, not Columbus, who first sets foot on the mainland of Central America.

Someone other than Vespucci himself most likely wrote the *Lettera*. Since the document does share some of the details of the familiar letters, it is safe to assume that the writer had read Vespucci's stories and based his work on that. Perhaps Vespucci even worked with an author to craft the *Lettera*, the way Marco Polo worked with Rustichello on his own tales. Yet the *Lettera* is clearly intended to discredit Columbus, and there is little reason to think that Vespucci ever wanted to do that.

Although many people have thought that Columbus and Vespucci were bitter enemies, the reverse is actually true. Not only did Vespucci plead to the Court of Spain for Columbus's titles to be restored, the two never contested each other's claims to the lands of the New World.

An Ongoing Mystery

Although the *Lettera* documented a competition between Vespucci and Columbus in the style of a tabloid newspaper, the two men, in fact, remained friendly throughout their lives. For example, Columbus, in 1505, in a letter to his son Ferdinand, wrote that Vespucci was "a very respectable man." It is highly unlikely that Vespucci himself would seek to discredit Columbus.

Still, the suggestion that someone might have beaten Columbus to his own discovery was exciting news for the public. Columbus and Vespucci were both celebrities of the time, as well as devoted admirers of each other's work. The *Lettera*, however, was another publishing success even with its grand lies. It was translated again and again, often with small variations between different editions.

In the end, it is difficult to know how to consider the *Lettera*. For centuries, it was the document most widely believed to be an accurate representation of Vespucci's travels. Without other sources of information to compare it to, scholars accused Vespucci of lying and stealing the glory from Columbus. And while Vespucci's reputation was rescued by the discovery of the familiar letters, the mystery remained.

For 200 years, *Mundus Novus* and the *Lettera* were considered authentic descriptions of Vespucci's explorations. After the familiar letters to Lorenzo di Pier Francesco de' Medici were discovered in the 1700s, experts began reexamining the documents. Without original copies, however, it was difficult to determine their accuracy. As late as the 1960s, historians dismissed those popular publications as exaggerations, but there is no proof that Vespucci didn't write them. In fact, we may never know.

What does seem certain is that the stories of Vespucci's explorations are the foundation of all the documents. Even if he did not write each one of them, they share too many details for any of them to be completely false. And while it is entirely possible that other authors exaggerated the truth of Vespucci's journeys, he was, in fact, the first explorer to understand what he was seeing. He was the first to realize that an entirely unknown continent existed in the ocean between Europe and Asia.

4

A VOYAGE FOR SPAIN

And the present letter is to give you the news that I returned about one month ago from the Indian regions, brought safely back by the grace of God to this, the city of Seville.
—Letter from Vespucci to Lorenzo di Pier
Francesco de' Medici, July 18, 1500

According to his letters to Lorenzo di Pier Francesco de' Medici, Vespucci sailed from the Spanish city of Cadiz on May 18, 1499. King Ferdinand V of Spain sent the expedition in hopes of finding treasure in the New World. The king had been disappointed during the previous year when Columbus returned to Spain from what was now his third voyage to the New World without large quantities of gold or silver.

Alonso de Ojeda and Juan de la Cosa were captain and pilot of Vespucci's expedition. Vespucci's duties included cartography and astronomy. Vespucci's letters mention two ships, but other records suggest that there were four ships in all. It is likely that Vespucci was in charge of two ships for exploration, while de Hojeda used two others to search for treasure.

"I departed with two caravels," Vespucci wrote, "and set my course along the African coast." The ships sailed along the western coastline of Africa before heading southwest across the Atlantic Ocean toward the New World. For more than three weeks, the sailors saw nothing but sea. After twenty-four days, they finally spotted land in the distance, in what is now the South American country of Guyana.

Strange New World

Vespucci and his crew members anchored their massive ships at sea and used smaller boats to paddle closely along the shoreline. The air closer to the coast was richly scented. What they saw amazed them. The land was thick with strange trees, which grew right to the edge of the water. All the limbs and roots grew together, creating a pattern that enclosed the forest. It was quite beautiful. Vespucci wrote that the strange sights and new smells were "so soothing" that it had "quite a restorative effect" on his crew.

Vespucci, one of the foremost navigators of his day, would later be appointed chief pilot for Spain. He had sailed from the Spanish city of Cadiz, which is shown in this illustration, in 1499. His objective was to explore the New World and to report his findings directly to the king and queen of Spain, which he did in his letters filled with eloquent observations about a strange new land and its native people.

The freshwater along the coast was suitable for drinking, so the men refilled the ship's drinking supplies. In the days that followed, Vespucci learned that the freshwater came from enormous rivers that emptied into the Atlantic Ocean. Vespucci was probably the first European explorer to enter the enormous Amazon River, as he searched for a safe port.

Finding nowhere near the coast to anchor the large ships, the expedition sailed farther south. Vespucci, like Columbus, believed that he was sailing along the eastern coast of India. He searched for Cape Catigarra, a landmark of the Indian coast that was indicated on Ptolemy's map of the world. In order to find his position, Vespucci used calculations called latitude and longitude.

Sailors could estimate their north-south position by watching the North Star at night. The North Star is almost directly above the earth's North Pole. As a ship traveled farther south, the North Star appeared lower in the sky. Map lines, known as parallels, indicating latitude were shown as circles around the globe. Vespucci struggled with a way to map his distance east and west. He developed a series of measurements based on the cycles of the moon. These were mapped out using lines that ran from one pole to the other. These lines became known as meridians. Latitude and longitude were both expressed in degrees, units of measurement that indicated distance from the equator (in latitude) or the prime meridian (in longitude).

Spanish and Portuguese exploratory ships, like the ones shown here, were mostly caravels with smooth-sided planks fitted closely together. Although the inside was of solid construction, they often leaked. Vespucci, who had more than once dealt with *teredos*, or shipworms, that would eat the hulls of his ships, later outfitted his vessels with a lead coating.

Vespucci estimated the position of his ships using his skills as both a mapmaker and an astronomer. He knew his ships were in the Tropic Zone, and he was able to keep track of his distance from the equator. By day, he confirmed his measurements by the position of the sun, which rose directly above the ships at noon. "Sometimes for an hour or two in the course of the day we had no shadow," he wrote. Vespucci disputed the European myth that the Tropic Zone was too hot for human life to survive. In fact, he found that "the air is fresher and more temperate" in the Tropic Zone.

At night, he charted the stars and planets of the Southern Hemisphere. Vespucci saw the Southern Cross and other constellations that were not visible in Europe. He hoped to locate a star in the southern skies that would act as a navigational tool, the way the North Star was traditionally used by navigators in the Northern Hemisphere.

Meeting the Cannibals

Periodically, Vespucci and his men went ashore using the smaller boats. They attempted to explore the new land on foot but made little progress because of the dense forests. They observed parrots and other colorful birds, exotic flowers and fruits, and unfamiliar breeds of fish and sea life. They also

The Republic of Trinidad and Tobago was originally populated by the Igneri, a relatively peaceful people, and also by the cannibal Caraïbes, who Vespucci likely encountered. Trinidad was discovered by Columbus in 1498 and the Spaniards established a colony on the island in 1577, but English explorer Sir Walter Raleigh destroyed the settlement in 1595.

saw signs of human life, but for many weeks they encountered no indigenous people.

When the expedition failed to find a suitable port for its ships after sailing south for several days, Vespucci directed them to turn around and search in the other direction. Eventually, after sailing northeast away from the mainland, they came to the island of Trinidad, named only one year earlier by Columbus in honor of the Holy Trinity.

As they approached the island, Vespucci saw native people gathering near the shore observing his ships. After making careful preparations for battle in case fighting was necessary, Vespucci went ashore with several other men. But just as they set foot on Trinidad's beaches, the native people quickly fled into the jungle. Using sign language, Vespucci slowly managed to convince the people of Trinidad that he had come in peace.

The natives were completely nude, a concept that shocked Vespucci and his men, who were deeply religious and believed that immodesty was sinful. Still, Vespucci was open to different customs and he understood that people from foreign lands were bound to live differently.

He and his men were able to learn more about the natives by communicating with sign language. The process of communication was gradual, but the natives showed them their shields and arrows and took them to their village, where Vespucci and his men were fed a traditional meal of tropical fruit. The Europeans were disturbed, however, to learn that the island natives were cannibals, or people who sometimes ate the flesh of other human beings. Vespucci briefly described the practice in his letters. "They do not eat one another," he wrote. "They go in search of prey from races that are different from them."

After returning to the ships, the expedition sailed back to the coast of the mainland. In the Gulf of Paria (named by Christopher Columbus just the year before), the expedition came to a large village built on the beach. The people of the village welcomed the Europeans, and again Vespucci and his men were treated to a meal. The villagers also gave the Europeans pearls and parrots to take home to Spain. These people were of a different tribe than the cannibals and spoke a different language.

Vespucci visited a place he called the Island of the Giants (which was probably the South American island now known as Curaçao). As they explored its land, Vespucci's men followed a footpath that led to a small village several miles away. Once there, they encountered seven women who were much taller than any of the European men. Vespucci's men decided to kidnap two of the giant women to take back as gifts for King Ferdinand. They quickly had a change of heart when thirty-six male villagers appeared carrying weapons.

Vespucci described the male villagers as taller than the women, and they carried bows, arrows, and clubs. The Europeans were frightened by the size of their hosts but used sign language to indicate that they were peaceful. Vespucci ordered his men to return to the ships, escorted by the massive people.

Amerigo Vespucci called Curaçao "Isla de los Gigantes" (Island of the Giants) because the Arawak Indians who lived there were so tall and slender. As it sits just off the coast of Venezuela, Curaçao has historically been a crossroads for expeditions. In the 1600s, the island was a staging ground for colonial wars and, later, pirates sought shelter in its deepwater ports.

Battles in the Name of God

Not all of Vespucci's encounters with indigenous people were peaceful. As the expedition continued sailing along the coast of what is now South America, it encountered tribes who were less than welcoming. Vespucci and his crew were frequently attacked in the small boats they used to go ashore.

Though his men were often far outnumbered, their metal swords were more effective weapons than the native arrows and shields. And because the natives wore no clothing or protective gear, many of them died from their wounds. Only two members of Vespucci's crew died in battle, even though they fought against many native warriors.

Even in the fiercest conflicts, Vespucci's men believed they were doing God's work. Their religious convictions led them to slaughter hundreds of native people. Even worse, they often followed a winning battle by burning down the enemies' shelters. Though Vespucci was a Christian and shared the religious convictions of his crew, his views were more progressive. He was not obsessed with converting natives to Christianity and does not seem to have provoked conflicts with other people unless he and his men were attacked first. This was quite a contrast to many other European explorers of the time, who firmly believed it was their sacred duty to save natives' souls, or kill them in trying to do so.

Vespucci was surprised that none of the native people whom he encountered possessed gold or silver. Some were generous with gifts of crystal and pearls, but these items had little worth for the king of Spain. Vespucci, like Columbus, was still convinced that he was exploring parts of India, and he expected to find the treasure that country was famed for.

He didn't neglect to notice that the lands were abundant in natural resources. He made notes about different kinds of wood, cotton, and food that would be useful to European nations. He remained amazed by the land's beautiful aromas and colors. In one village, he saw native houses that reminded him of the Italian city of Venice and began referring to the area as Venezuela, a name that means "Little Venice."

After nearly a year at sea, Vespucci's expedition then sailed to the island of Hispaniola, which Columbus had settled six years earlier. Once there, the expedition rested for two months, restocking supplies and repairing ships. Afterward, the expedition sailed north and explored the islands of the Bahamas for the purpose of capturing slaves, the revenues from which were needed to pay for the voyage.

Vespucci boasted that he "discovered more than a thousand islands" in the Bahamas, though this seems unlikely since the crew was tired and homesick. Vespucci's men fought

The First Voyage?

According to both the *Mundus Novus* and the *Lettera*, Vespucci led two expeditions for Spain. The *Lettera* describes a first Spanish expedition in 1497, separate from the voyage of 1499. There are many conflicting details in the the *Lettera*'s description of Vespucci's "first voyage" giving historians many reasons to be skeptical about its contents. It is far more a work of storytelling than of science.

While describing a visit to the island of "Iti" (Haiti, which Columbus had named Hispaniola), the *Lettera* uses latitudes of the coastline as far north as Chesapeake Bay, Virginia. The *Lettera* also tells of sailing around what was later known as the Gulf of Mexico, and going ashore on the peninsula later known as Florida.

Vespucci was extremely careful with his measurements of latitude and longitude. Because he was desperately trying to make sense of Ptolemy's world map, he knew that his calculations needed to be precise. It seems unlikely that he would write about one location while carelessly identifying it with the wrong latitude. It's more likely that someone who was interested in causing trouble for Columbus wrote the *Lettera*.

frequent battles with native people during this period. More than 200 natives were captured in battle. Vespucci wrote, according to Luciano Formisano in his book, *Letters from a New World: Amerigo Vespucci's Discovery of America*, "and we did with them whatever we wished." Those who did not die at sea were sold as slaves when the crew returned to Spain.

Home at Last

The expedition finally returned home to Cadiz in June 1500. Once ashore, Vespucci met with King Ferdinand and Queen Isabella and told them of his journey. He presented the queen with the pearls and other gemstones he had been given.

During the next several months, Vespucci lived peacefully in Seville. He began to experience periodic fevers and chills, which would plague him for the rest of his life, probably a form of sleeping sickness or another parasitic tropical disease like malaria. His illness never kept him far from adventure, though. In 1501, King Manuel of Portugal requested a meeting with Vespucci. He was about to set sail again.

Vespucci must have been relieved to return to Seville, which is pictured in this illustration. Seville was important in history as a center of cultural activity, one of the leading cities of Muslim Spain, and the base of Spanish exploration of the New World. Seville houses the Torre del Oro (the Golden Tower) built by a former Muslim ruler but used as a landing depot for bullion from the Americas. Today the tower is a naval museum.

5
A VOYAGE FOR PORTUGAL

I count this all as time well spent, for I hope to be famous for many an age, if I return safe and sound from this voyage . . .
—Letter from Vespucci to Lorenzo di Pier
Francesco de' Medici, June 4, 1501

At the time of Columbus's voyages, Spain and Portugal agreed to divide ownership of the lands discovered in the New World. However, during Vespucci's voyage for Spain in 1499, he understood that his expedition had crossed into waters that had technically been claimed for Portugal. Vespucci feared that King Manuel might punish him for taking Spanish ships into Portuguese waters. Fortunately, he had no need to worry. King Manuel knew of Vespucci's skill as a navigator. In fact, he wanted Vespucci to lead an expedition for Portugal.

This undated photo shows the first page of a letter written by Portuguese scribe Pedro Vaz de Caminha and announces the discovery of Brazil on April 22, 1500, by Pedro Álvares Cabral. The letter was addressed to King Manuel I and is considered Brazil's "birth certificate."

posto q̃ o capitam moor desta vossa frota e asi os
outros capitães screuam a vossa alteza a noua do acha
mento desta vossa terra noua que ora nesta nauy
gação achou nom leixarey tambem de dar disso
minha conta a vossa alteza asy como eu milhor
poder ajnda que pera bem contar e falar o pu[r]
sa[ber] que todos fazem pyor q̃ tome vossa alteza minha
jnoramça por boõ voontade. a qual bem certo cra
e a se meu contar nem a [a]fremosear [a] aqui de fre[mo]
sura quem por em [por] vy me [por] pareçer / da naueg[a]
çam, screuerad durão [a] [de] [a]mais [que] eu darey aqui o
tu a vossa alteza de que non sabere fazer [e]sob
[a]que[s]to [men] [ter] [a]tu de verdade [a] [por] tanto Snõr
o q̃ ey de falar [a] começo e digo

que a [parti]da de [bel]em como vossa alteza sabe foy seg[un]
dafeira [que] [fora] de março. e [sabado] [dez]ij do dito mes [a]tan[tos]
os bixij [q̃] [ao] oras nõ achamos antre as canarias
[a]mayo [a] por [de] da gram canarea [a] ali andamos [a] de
[aquel]e dia [en] calma al[g]ûs de las oyto de tres ou
quatro legoas. [e] domingo xxij do dito mes [a]c[a]s
[a] oras pouco mais ou menos ouuemos vista dos [los]
[ve]rdes [a] [de] s. [da]sto [de] [por] nycolao [se]g[un]do dito [do] [por]
[se]u voto pelos sanoure [seguy]nt [a]s[por]ment [per][a] [da] frota [cha]
[a]mançeteos [e] pedro da frota uaã [se]o [da]nte[s]es [de] [von]
[e] sua naão [seu] hy auez tempo forte no [on] [tra]yo
[por] [a] poder ter [a]... [a] [os] capitães suas [di]ligençias [p]a[ra]
[a]char [a]chados[e] [as] [os] outros partes [a] nõ pareçeram [mais]
[e] asi [se]g[uy]mos [n]osu ramino por [o]ficiual [de] lon[go]
[a]tee [ter]ça feira [di]tauos [a] pascoa que [fo]ram vijt
dias dabril que topamos al[g]uûs [si]gnaães de trra
[fi]m[p]da dita [por] [xij] [as] os pilotos [de]zi[a]m[obra] [de]
bj lho ou [lxx] legoas: vos e[n]quaes heram nauta uau
[fe]dade de [rui]s compridas [a]qui[r] os naçe[an]ços [a]
[cham]a botello [a]asi outros [a]que tam bem chama
uad dasno / [a]a quarta feira [se]guynte pola ma...

Setting sail from Lisbon on May 13, 1501, Vespucci did just that. His expedition of three ships was to follow the entire path of the coastline he had discovered on the previous voyage. Still strong in his conviction that he had been exploring the eastern coast of Asia, Vespucci carefully studied existing maps of the world. He felt certain he could retrace the coastline he found on Ptolemy's ancient map.

Cabral's Journey

Vespucci's expedition first sailed south to an island off the coast of Cape Verde, on the western coast of Africa near present-day Dakar, Senegal. Once there, Vespucci encountered another Portuguese expedition returning to Lisbon from India. Pedro Álvares Cabral, the captain of that Indian expedition, was reluctant to reveal information about his experiences in India. The report of his trip was considered top secret because King Manuel was eager to claim Indian lands visited by Cabral in the name of Portugal. Despite the secrecy, Vespucci learned about Cabral's journey from other members of that expedition.

Cabral's expedition had departed from Lisbon on March 9, 1500, with fourteen ships. Together they sailed south to Cape Verde and then southwest toward the New World. Like Columbus and Vespucci before him,

Cabral expected to reach Asia by sailing west. With Cabral at the helm of the secret mission, his crew sighted land on April 22, as his fleet approached the coast of what is now Brazil. Claiming the land for Portugal, Cabral erected a cross and named the spot Santa Cruz. Not surprisingly, Cabral and his men encountered people in the strange new land who were unclothed, as Vespucci had described. There was little doubt that Cabral and Vespucci had visited the same area of the world.

Cabral's expedition left Santa Cruz and sailed north to restock supplies of wood and fresh water. Afterward, Cabral turned his fleet in a southeastern direction toward the southern tip of Africa. Eventually, he and his crew sailed around Africa's mighty Cape of Good Hope toward India.

Taprobana and Catigarra

Ptolemy's map of the world included an island called Taprobana located just off the coast of India. Vespucci, curious about Ptolemy's accuracy, wanted to know if Cabral's men had encountered such an island, but they didn't recognize the name. They did know of an island named Ceylon (Sri Lanka) that was separated from the southern tip of India by a strait of water, and described another island even farther east named Sumatra, which also resembled Taprobana.

Vespucci also questioned Cabral's men about Cape Catigarra, which according to Ptolemy's map was located near the easternmost edge of Asia. On his own expedition for Spain in 1499, Vespucci had tried to find Cape Catigarra without success. Cabral's men had not heard the name Catigarra before, and their descriptions of the places they had visited did not match those on Ptolemy's map.

Instead, Cabral's men told Vespucci about Asian cities rich with precious gold, exotic spices, and beautiful fabrics. They described Asian junks—gigantic Asian ships used for transporting large quantities of food and animals, even elephants! Yet nothing they had experienced in Asia was remotely like the people they had encountered near Santa Cruz.

Vespucci made notes about the new information that he learned from Cabral's men. While still in Cape Verde, Vespucci wrote a letter to Lorenzo di Pier Francesco de' Medici detailing his understanding of Cabral's secret expedition. Vespucci told Medici that he "had very lengthy conversations" with Cabral's men about "the coast of the land along which they had run."

This map shows the western coast of Africa, part of a region also known as the Sahel. Vespucci's expedition first sailed south to Cape Verde, a port on its western coast near present-day Dakar, Senegal.

This 1560 portolan (nautical) chart of North Africa (present-day Morocco) shows the Canary Islands, Cape Verde, the Strait of Gibraltar, and the southern coasts of Portugal and Spain.

Vespucci was disappointed that Cabral's expedition did not have any mathematicians aboard who could calculate longitude. Without those calculations, Vespucci was not able to accurately compare his own discoveries with those of Cabral. Vespucci was one of only a few men at the time who understood how to calculate longitude. At a loss, he tried his best to estimate the figures he needed based on the stories of Cabral's men.

Heaven on Earth

Vespucci's expedition left Cape Verde and sailed southwest. He plotted a course that brought his expedition farther south than his first voyage. This voyage across the Atlantic Ocean took much longer than it had before, most likely due to a series of storms and unfavorable winds that were detailed in *Mundus Novus*. By August, more than two months after leaving Cape Verde, Vespucci finally sighted land. He and his crew arrived at a location they called the Cape of San Roque on the easternmost coast of Brazil. In another letter to his friend Lorenzo Medici, Vespucci again described its lush greenery. "The fields produce many sweet and delicious herbs," he wrote. "Sometimes I marveled so much at the delicate scents of the herbs and flowers, and the tastes of those fruits and roots, that

Flying dragons were among the creatures reportedly seen by Vespucci and other explorers in the New World. This illustration is one of many to be found in the famous sixteenth-century books created by Theodor de Bry. De Bry is best known for his series of volumes chronicling expeditions to the Americas.

I thought I must be near the Earthly Paradise." Vespucci was also impressed with the different variations of animals he saw, including "lynxes, baboons, monkeys of many kinds, and many large snakes." He wrote, "I think so many kinds could not have fit into Noah's ark."

The records that Vespucci kept of his positions both on land and at sea were meticulous. And even though measurements of latitude were quite common and relatively easy to track, longitude always challenged even the most talented navigator. Indicating these distances east or west from the equator required translating the distance a ship traveled in leagues (one league is between 2.4 and 4.6 miles) to the degrees that represented those distances on a map. Vespucci used these calculations to sort out which lands belonged to Portugal and which belonged to Spain.

Portugal's agreement with Spain allowed it to claim land as far as 370 leagues (about 1,500 miles) west of the Cape Verde Islands. By Vespucci's measurements, this entitled Portugal to a piece of the land he was already exploring, including the Cape of San Roque. Vespucci set out to identify a line of demarcation that separated Portuguese and Spanish territories. With great skill, Vespucci managed to map the line of demarcation accurately. When compared to modern measurements, his estimate was accurate to within two miles of where it should have been.

Even more incredible were Vespucci's estimates of the size of the earth. Ptolemy and Toscanelli had calculated its circumference as approximately 22,500 miles around. After making his discovery of "the Indies," Columbus had boasted that, in fact, the globe was smaller, about 20,000 miles around. Vespucci, however, had gathered more information on his previous voyage. He was able to use the stories of Cabral's expedition to expand his understanding of the earth's size. Then, while making calculations that accounted for the celestial cycles of the stars and the moon, Vespucci stumbled onto a surprising discovery. The earth, in fact, was much larger than believed, nearly 25,000 miles around.

Now Vespucci knew what other explorers had not known. The distance between Europe and Asia was much greater than they had ever believed. The expanse was so large that it was quite possible that another body of land existed between the two continents.

Cultural Observation

Besides being a careful navigator and geographical interpreter, Vespucci spent his time reporting about the condition of the lands he traveled as well as detailed information about the native people. For example, he went into the jungle and spent three weeks living with natives there, most likely members of the Tupi-Guarani linguistic group of Brazil. They had light-colored skin, little body hair, and, like some of the other indigenous people of the region, were cannibals. Still, Vespucci's goal was to observe them and accurately record what he witnessed. Remarkably, he did not run in fear or pass judgment on their unusual customs.

Vespucci, on the deck of the ship, is shown approaching the New World. The figures rising from the sea may represent the deities and monsters thought to inhabit unexplored areas of the sea.

AMERI. VESPVC.

Instead, Vespucci took careful notes about their customs. He was amazed that they could build such strong huts without the use of metal. "I have seen houses longer than 200 paces and 30 paces wide, most skillfully built," he wrote. He also saw hammocks for the first time, which the natives wove from cotton. These textiles were used as comfortable sleeping quarters. Vespucci described the people as "warlike" and "very cruel," yet if his letter to Lorenzo Medici is correct, he had no violent interactions with them during his stay.

Vespucci also described the ways in which they decorated their bodies. To appear more frightening, they poked holes in the skin of their lips and cheeks, into which they inserted pieces of bone and colored stone. They did not have marriages in the European sense, and the men had relationships with many women in the tribe. Vespucci knew of one native man with ten wives. If they went to battle with other tribes, women were sometimes captured as slaves.

The women also appeared to have no difficulty in giving birth. "The very same day they go off to the fields to wash themselves, and they barely suffer in childbirth," Vespucci wrote. He was disturbed by "a certain diabolical fury" that came over some of the native men. At these moments, they gathered their families to witness the ceremonial killing of one of the wives and all the children she had given birth to.

Most frightening was the practice of eating other human beings. "This is certain, for in their houses we found human flesh hung up for smoking, and a lot of it." Vespucci expressed his anger at their acts of cannibalism, but he wasn't sure if they understood his disapproval. He did manage to buy ten slaves from the natives—men that would have been eaten—but he did not indicate what became of those people. After going back to Vespucci's ships, they may have been sold as slaves.

Vespucci longed to understand why the cannibals fought with each other. According to information found in Formisano's book *Letters from a New World*, "They do not have private property, or command empires or kingdoms, and have no notion of greed . . . for things or for power." Yet the answer was beyond European reasoning: The only explanation the natives had was that they had fought with one another "since ancient times."

Still, some of the conflicts described by Vespucci's letters seem exaggerated or even unbelievable. For example, the *Lettera* includes a story of some of Vespucci's crew being attacked. According to this version, two members went ashore and followed a group of natives into the jungle. When the men failed to return, a third crew member went ashore using sign language to communicate with the native women. Vespucci, watching from the ships, saw the third young man being clubbed to

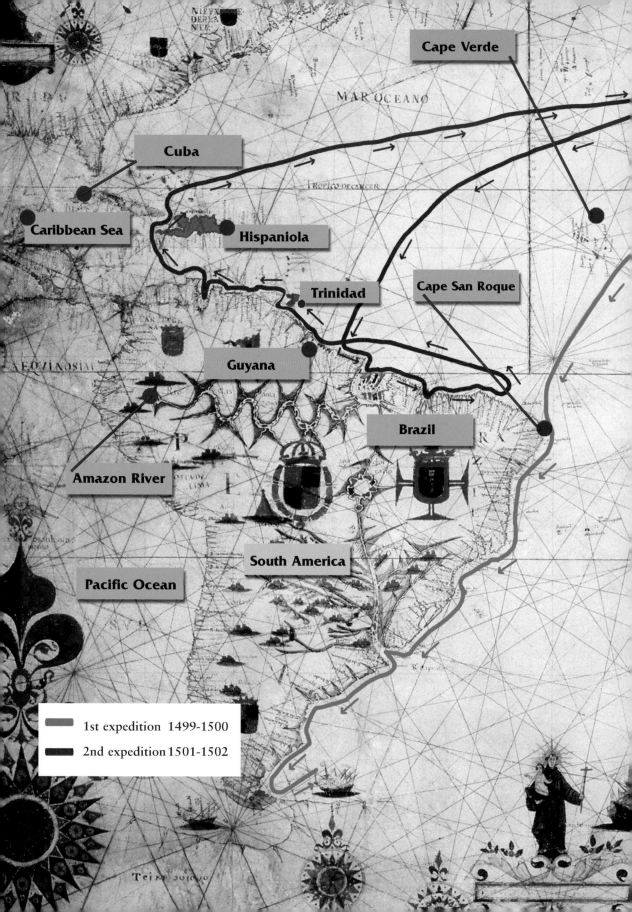

Cape Verde

Cuba

Caribbean Sea

Hispaniola

Cape San Roque

Trinidad

Guyana

Brazil

Amazon River

South America

Pacific Ocean

1st expedition 1499-1500

2nd expedition 1501-1502

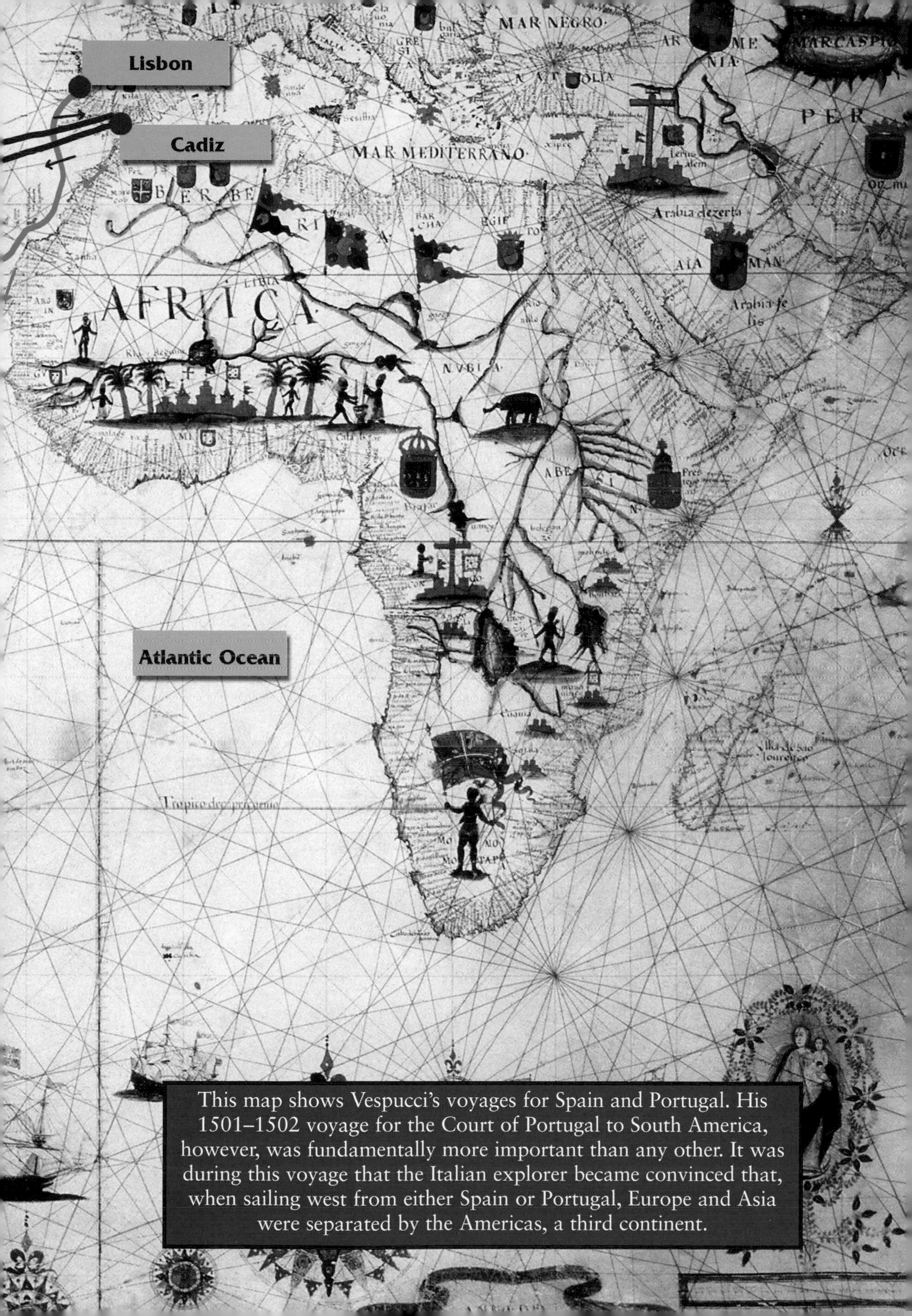

Lisbon
Cadiz
Atlantic Ocean
MAR NEGRO
MAR MEDITERRANO
AFRICA
NVBIA
Arabia dezerta
Tropico de capricornio

This map shows Vespucci's voyages for Spain and Portugal. His 1501–1502 voyage for the Court of Portugal to South America, however, was fundamentally more important than any other. It was during this voyage that the Italian explorer became convinced that, when sailing west from either Spain or Portugal, Europe and Asia were separated by the Americas, a third continent.

death and dragged deeper into the jungle. Meanwhile, the natives built an enormous fire on a mountainside. While Vespucci and his men watched helplessly from their ships, the natives tore apart the bodies of the three Europeans, roasted them, and ate them. It's a dramatic and frightening story, but it conflicts with other accounts that indicate that all of Vespucci's men arrived home safely.

Rethinking the Shape of Things

After three weeks, Vespucci left the Tupi-Guarani and returned to his ships. He now doubted that he was exploring Asia, but he needed to prove his theory. Vespucci decided to continue following the coastline in a southerly direction. If he were in Asia, he supposed, then he should eventually find Cape Catigarra as it appeared on Ptolemy's map. He was also searching for a water route that crossed Asia's mainland.

Through the fall and winter of 1501, Vespucci's expedition continued sailing in a southern direction. Vespucci, keeping careful track of his longitude, mapped the unfamiliar coastline. As the ships sailed still farther south, he watched new constellations rise in the night sky, which he drew as well.

From information that he derived from his calculations and mapmaking, Vespucci was now certain that he was not in Asia. His expedition was sailing close to fifty degrees south of the equator, which was nearly as far south as Africa's southern tip, a place later named the Cape of Good Hope. Ptolemy's map gave no indication that any parts of Asia extended so far south. Eventually the weather turned extremely cold, and Vespucci no longer saw any signs of human life. At last, the rough weather forced the expedition to return home in March 1502.

On the return voyage, the ships stopped at Sierra Leone, Africa, to restock with fresh water and other supplies and to gain some much-needed rest. The *Lettera* states that one of the three ships was also destroyed there after suffering terrible damage. After two weeks, the expedition continued, stopping briefly in the Azore Islands before finally arriving in Lisbon, Portugal, by September.

6

RETURN TO FAME

No one shall go in the . . . ships as pilots, nor receive pay as pilots, nor may the masters receive them on board ship, until they have first been examined by you, Amerigo Vespucci, our Chief Pilot, and they shall be given by you a certificate of examination and approval.
—From the document appointing Vespucci
chief pilot of Spain, 1508

Vespucci returned to Lisbon with his incredible news. He met immediately with King Manuel to tell him of the scope of his travels. He exchanged ideas with Portuguese mapmakers and scientists, so that they could revise their maps and measurements of the earth's circumference. Based on his calculations of latitude and longitude, and his knowledge of the distances traveled by his ships, Vespucci spoke with confidence about his theory that the world was much larger than educated men had previously thought.

Just four years after King Ferdinand had named Vespucci chief pilot of Spain, historians believe he died from malaria, a disease he contracted during one of his voyages. The accounts of his journeys to the Americas, however, would live on to tell his tale. Those publications, including *Mundus Novus* of 1502, appealed to three times as many readers as did books that detailed Columbus's voyages from the same period.

News of Vespucci's discoveries traveled quickly. Within the year, most Europeans had heard that an entirely unknown continent lay between Europe and Asia. The discovery of new lands brought excitement at the thought of new settlements and trade routes. At the time, there was still great hope that the New World would be a greater supplier of gold, silver, and other wealth.

But Vespucci was exhausted. He was in poor health and had fevers and chills. Many experts and historians believe he may have suffered from malaria, most likely caught from his earlier travels in South America. After finishing his business in Portugal, Vespucci returned home to Seville, Spain, late in 1502. Once back in Spain, Vespucci married a Spanish woman named Maria Cerezo, although conflicting reports say that his marriage occurred earlier, perhaps in 1498. They lived together happily along with Vespucci's nephew Giovanni.

There are other documents that suggest that Vespucci did plan to sail again for Spain, however. Those records indicated that this voyage, scheduled for late 1506, never took place. Instead, Vespucci remained in Spain detailing his maps and new calculations.

World leaders had the highest respect for Vespucci after he returned from the Portuguese expedition. King Ferdinand named Vespucci the chief pilot of Spain in March 1508. His duties put him in charge of navigational

A Final Voyage?

Again, the *Lettera* confuses things by suggesting that Vespucci took a fourth voyage, sailing for Portugal in 1503, but no reports exist to verify this journey.

According to the *Lettera*, Vespucci left Lisbon on May 10, 1503. The expedition sailed again to the Cape Verde Islands and stocked supplies. The unnamed captain of the expedition then decided to sail south to Sierra Leone, "for no good reason at all." Terrible storms prevented the ships from landing in Sierra Leone and conveniently prevented anyone in that country from confirming the story.

After sailing southwest toward the New World, the expedition found "the island of ill luck for the entire fleet." One of the ships was wrecked. The other crewmen went ashore, where they encountered natives and built a fort. Vespucci headed for home, leaving twenty-four men on the island. The expedition returned to Lisbon on June 18, 1504.

When compared, this description of Vespucci's "final" trip sounds like voyages made by Columbus in 1492 and 1503. Other sources confirm that Vespucci was already home in Seville by 1503. While this story makes for enjoyable reading, it's doubtful that Vespucci would have undertaken the trip. In 1503, Vespucci was fifty-two years old and in poor health. He had been offered Spanish citizenship and was well regarded by the Spanish king, giving him plenty of reasons to stay at home with his wife and nephew.

training in the country, and he began teaching navigation to students of his own, including Giovanni. Vespucci's students took lessons from him at his house. Most important, it was Vespucci who decided when they were skilled enough to set sail. This meant that every new navigator had to learn the difficult art of calculating longitude, an important advancement for future Spanish sailors.

Vespucci, also in charge of Spain's official world maps, updated them whenever sailors returned with details about the New World. His new position came with a handsome salary, allowing him to live out the rest of his life in great comfort. And though he never returned to Italy, Vespucci's home city of Florence also celebrated his achievements in lavish ceremonies and festivals. His family members also received special honors because of their relation to the great explorer.

Tributes and Accusations

There was soon a European demand to revise all world maps to reflect the discoveries of Columbus and Vespucci. Just as Vespucci had done, many cartographers planned to update their maps that had been historically based on Ptolemy's *Geography*. Martin Waldseemüller, a German geography professor, combined a revised world map with a Latin translation of the *Lettera* to create his *Introduction to Cosmography*.

Waldseemüller drew his map to match Ptolemy's *Geography* in many respects, but he used Vespucci's calculations for drawing the New World. As he drew the finishing details on his elaborate map, he found that he needed a name for the new continent. Using the Latin translation of Vespucci's first name, he called the new continent America. Waldseemüller's map was published in 1507, but there is no proof that Vespucci was aware that the new continent had been named in his honor. Vespucci, survived by his wife, Maria, died in Seville on February 22, 1512, just five years later. His nephew Giovanni later became a successful navigator.

Though Waldseemüller had not intended the name America as an insult to Columbus, the name caused problems for centuries. Columbus had "discovered" it first, and many people felt the new continent should be named after him instead. Additionally, supporters of Columbus were outraged by the publication of the *Lettera*, which suggested that Vespucci had set foot on the mainland before Columbus did. Since Vespucci supposedly wrote the *Lettera*, many people now spoke out against him. They accused him of jealousy and said that he had named the new continent after himself.

This world map, on the next two pages, issued by German publisher and cartographer Martin Waldseemüller in 1507, was the first to label the southern lands in the New World "America." Later, when it became clear that the Americas, North and South, were one great landmass, Vespucci's name was used for the whole continent. The book that published the map of the Americas was so popular that a second edition was printed six months later.

During his lifetime, Vespucci had little control over the exaggerated use of his stories and his name. After his death, however, the exaggerations worsened. Accusations against Vespucci came from respected professionals as well as fellow explorers. In nearly every case, these people had no way of knowing that Vespucci did not name the new continent after himself. It was not until 1900 that a scholar proved that it was Waldseemüller, not Vespucci, who had named South America.

The letters to Medici were discovered hundreds of years after Vespucci's death. In the meantime, most people accepted that it was he who had written the exaggerated *Mundus Novus* and the *Lettera*. A Dominican priest, Bartolome de Las Casas, filed a harsh objection to Vespucci's work in the 1500s. Las Casas was associated with the Columbus family, who felt hurt by the *Lettera*'s claim that Vespucci had been the first to set foot on the mainland.

"It is well here to consider the injury and injustice that Amerigo Vespucci appears to have done to [Columbus]," Las Casas wrote. "What Amerigo has written to make himself famous and give himself credit . . . was done with intention." This was only the beginning. Over the next centuries, many educated and respected men stepped forward to accuse Vespucci of lying. During the 1800s, even the famed American writer Ralph Waldo Emerson wrote that Vespucci "managed to baptize half the earth with his own dishonest name!"

Changing the World Forever

The accusations that Vespucci lied about his life and discoveries damaged his reputation. The words of Las Casas and others like him were used to discredit Vespucci even after the discovery of the Medici letters. Fortunately, later historians began to review all the documents available.

During the late 1800s, when the Medici letters were published for the first time, scholars found a map drawn by Juan de la Cosa in 1500. De la Cosa had been a pilot for voyages of both Columbus and Vespucci. The map showed the coastline of North America as far north as North Carolina. The map also showed Florida and the island of Cuba. It was the first time scholars had any evidence that Europeans had knowledge of that part of the American coastline. Perhaps Vespucci really did take the first and last voyages described in the *Lettera*. However, until further documentation is discovered, it remains impossible to prove.

The various letters and documents associated with Vespucci are puzzling indeed. We may never know whether they provide us with a complete picture of Vespucci. Yet they still reveal the work of a brilliant human being. Vespucci expanded the understanding of the world through his careful, detailed explorations. He accurately mapped portions of the world that had never been seen by European eyes. He perfected the method

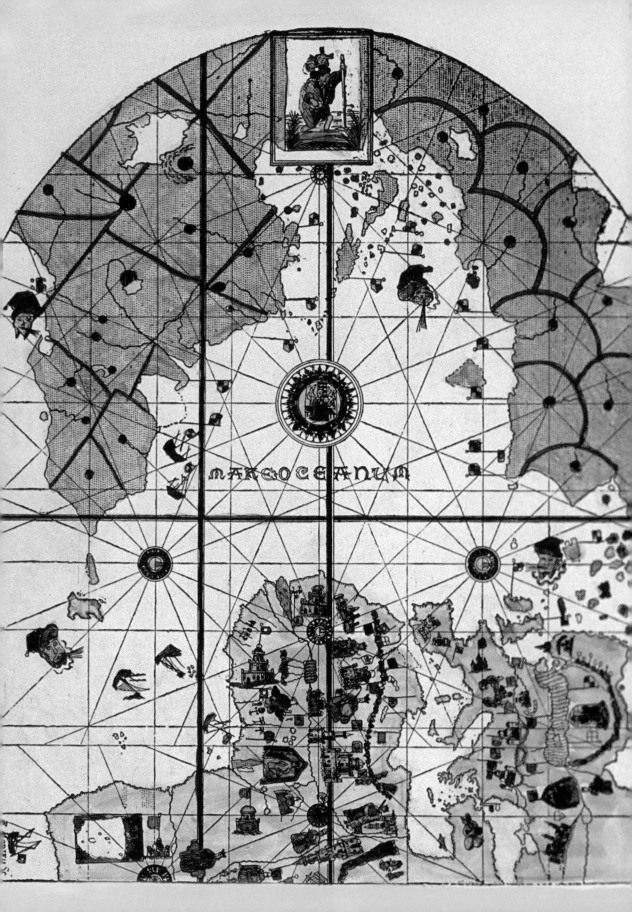

MARE OCEANVM

of determining longitude, and he calculated the circumference of the earth far more accurately than anyone had before him.

Perhaps even more important, Vespucci approached his explorations with a willingness to experience new ideas and cultures. And unlike other explorers both before and after him, Vespucci's motivation to travel was based largely on his curiosity, not religion or greed. Though he did participate in killing many indigenous people on his first journey, he did so after first being attacked. This was a far different mind-set than the Spanish explorers who would follow him in the 1500s. Soldiers like Francisco Pizarro would go on to conquer South America with sheer force, slaughtering entire civilizations in the name of God and gold. While Vespucci was willing to merely observe native cultures, most European explorers who followed after him conquered land and enslaved people in the tradition of the Crusades.

There is little doubt that Vespucci was one of a kind. He was a rare combination of scientist, educator, and artist. He represented the very best qualities of the age of exploration. It is because of these reasons that many historians feel that the Americas were named in honor of the right man.

Although they are now badly faded, the outlines of Europe and Africa can be seen in the center of this map, drawn in 1500 by Christopher Columbus's pilot, Juan de la Cosa.

CHRONOLOGY

1451 Amerigo Vespucci is born in Florence, Italy, though some historians think he was actually born three years later.

1478 Vespucci moves to Paris to work as secretary to his uncle Guidoantonio.

1483 Vespucci begins working for the Medici family after the death of his father.

1491 Vespucci sails to Seville, Spain, on behalf of the Medici family.

1497 Vespucci's possible first voyage to the New World, perhaps reaching the Gulf of Mexico and Brazil.

1499   Vespucci's verified voyage for Spain. Reaches the coast of Guyana (and perhaps Brazil), sails into the Amazon River, and visits Aruba, Curaçao, Trinidad, and the Bahamas.

1501   Vespucci's verified voyage for Portugal. Sails south from Brazil along the coast of South America.

1503   Vespucci's possible fourth voyage, from Portugal to Brazil.

1507   A map of the New World, drawn by German mapmaker Martin Waldseemüller, is printed, naming present-day South America as "America" for the first time.

1508   Vespucci is named chief pilot of Spain.

1512   Vespucci dies in Seville, Spain.

GLOSSARY

ambassador   An official representative of one country who visits another country.

anonymous   Bearing or giving no name; of unknown authorship.

astrolabe   A tool used by navigators to measure the position of stars and planets.

astronomy   The science of the sun, moon, planets, and stars and their relationship to Earth.

calculate   To use mathematical methods to figure something out.

caravel   A small, light ship used by Spain and Portugal during the Renaissance.

cartography   The study of maps.

circumference   The distance around something circular.

constellation   A group of stars that have been given names.

continent   One of the seven great masses of land on the earth.

convert   To change religious beliefs.

cosmography   The ancient and ongoing study and drawing of the cosmos, or universe, and astronomy.

Crusades   Military expeditions authorized by the pope and undertaken by Christians in the eleventh, twelfth, and thirteenth centuries to recover the Holy Land from non-Christians.

diplomacy   The business of international relations.

equator   An imaginary line around the earth that separates it into two parts, north and south.

expedition   A trip for a special purpose, such as scientific study.

explorer   A person who travels to different places to learn more about them.

geography   The study of the earth's surface, climate, continents, countries, and people.

guild   An association of artisans.

hemisphere   Any half of the globe, usually called the Northern, Southern, Eastern, or Western Hemisphere.

humanism   The Renaissance philosophy focusing on the development of the individual, and the emphasis on secular (nonreligious) concerns.

immodesty   Indecency; something vulgar or shocking.

indigenous   Produced, growing, or living naturally in a country or climate; native.

latitude   Indicates position from north to south on the globe.

longitude   Indicates position from east to west on the globe.

merchants   People who buy and sell things for a living.

missive   A letter.

navigation   A way of figuring out which way a ship is headed.

pilot   A person who steers a ship.

quadrant   A tool used by navigators to measure the distance of stars and planets from the horizon.

rebel   To disobey the people or country in charge.

Renaissance   The period from the fourteenth to the sixteenth century when knowledge experienced a "rebirth" in Europe.

slavery   The system of one person "owning" another.

theory   An estimated guess based on limited information.

trade route   The path used to travel somewhere to buy and sell goods.

tribute   A gift or message of superiority or achievement.

unified   Two or more things that have been brought together as one thing.

FOR MORE INFORMATION

American Friends of the Hakluyt Society
The John Carter Brown Building
P.O. Box 1894
Providence, RI 02912
Web site: http://www.hakluyt.com

American Geographical Society
120 Wall Street, Suite 100
New York, NY 10005
(212) 422-5456
Web site: http://www.amergeog.org

The Mariners' Museum
100 Museum Drive
Newport News, VA 23606
(757) 596-2222
Web site: http://www.mariner.org

Web Sites

Due to the changing nature of Internet links, the Rosen Publishing Group, Inc., has developed an online list of Web sites related to the subject of this book. This site is updated regularly. Please use this link to access the list:

http://www.rosenlinks.com/lee/amve/

FOR FURTHER READING

Alper, Ann Fitzpatrick. *Forgotten Voyager: The Story of Amerigo Vespucci.* Minneapolis, MN: Carolrhoda Books, 1991.

Flowers, Sarah, ed. *The Age of Exploration* (World History Series). Farmington Hills, MI: Lucent Books, 1999.

Formisano, Luciano, ed. *Letters from a New World: Amerigo Vespucci's Discovery of America.* New York: Marsilio Publishers, 1992.

Fradin, Dennis Brindell. *Amerigo Vespucci.* New York: Franklin Watts, 1991.

Haywood, John. *Age of Discovery 1492 to 1815: World Atlas of the Past.* New York: Oxford University Press, 2000.

Miller, Heather. *Spain in the Age of Exploration* (Cultures of the Past). New York: Marshall Cavendish Corp, 1999.

BIBLIOGRAPHY

Baker, Nina Brown. *Amerigo Vespucci.*
   New York: Knopf, 1956.

Formisano, Luciano, ed. *Letters from a New World:
   Amerigo Vespucci's Discovery of America.*
   New York: Marsilio Publishers, 1992.

Knoop, Faith Yingling. *Amerigo Vespucci.*
   Champaign, IL: Garrard, 1966.

Markham, Clements R., trans. *The Letters of Amerigo
   Vespucci and Other Documents Illustrative of His
   Career.* London: The Hakluyt Society, 1894.

Microsoft Encarta Online Encyclopedia 2001. "Petrarch."
   Retrieved January 6, 2002 (http://encarta.msn.com).

Microsoft Encarta Online Encyclopedia 2001.
   "Marco Polo." Retrieved January 6, 2002
   (http://encarta.msn.com).

Microsoft Encarta Online Encyclopedia 2001.
   "Renaissance." Retrieved January 6, 2002
   (http://encarta.msn.com).

Pohl, Frederick Julius. *Amerigo Vespucci: Pilot Major.*
   New York: Octagon Books, 1966.

Syme, Ronald. *Amerigo Vespucci: Scientist and
   Sailor.* New York: William Morrow, 1969.

INDEX

A

Almagest, 10, 14
Amazon River, 56
astrolabe, 8

B

Berardi, Giannotto, 33, 38

C

Cabral, Pedro Álvares, 70–71, 73, 76, 79
cannibals/cannibalism, 6, 60, 61, 83, 86
Cape Catigarra, 56, 73, 86
Cape of San Roque, 76, 78
Christianity, 15, 16, 21, 63
Columbus, Christopher, 6, 20, 41, 49, 59, 61, 65, 93, 96
   friendship with Vespucci, 22, 51
   voyages/discoveries of, 5, 7, 18, 21–22, 33, 35, 36–40, 53, 56, 64, 68, 70, 78, 91, 92, 97
Cosa, Juan de la, 53, 97
Crusades, 15, 99
Cuba, 40, 97

D

Dark Ages, 14–16

E

Eriksson, Leif, 5

F

Ferdinand, king of Spain, 36, 40, 53, 61, 67, 90

G

Geography, 11, 14, 16, 22, 30, 35, 40, 92, 93
Gutenberg, Johannes, 18

H

Hispaniola, 38, 40, 64, 65
humanism, 16, 25, 29, 30

I

Indies, 5, 6, 35, 36, 78
Isabella, queen of Spain, 36, 67
Islam, 15, 16

K

Kublai Khan, 20, 40

L

La Isabela, 38, 40
latitude, 8, 38, 56, 65, 77–78, 88
Lettera, 48–49, 51, 52, 65, 83, 87, 91, 92, 93, 96, 97
longitude, 14, 38, 56, 65, 76, 78, 88, 92, 99

M

Manuel, king of Portugal, 67, 68, 70, 88
Medici, Lorenzo di Pier Francesco de', 31, 49
    letters to, 44, 45, 48, 49, 51, 52, 53, 73, 76, 82, 96, 97
Medici family, 25, 28, 31, 33
meridians, 56
Mundus Novus, 48, 49, 52, 65, 76, 96

O

Ojeda, Alonso de, 53

P

parallels, 56
Pizarro, Francisco, 99
Polo, Marco, 18–20, 40, 49
printing press, 18, 20, 44
Ptolemy, Claudius, 10–14, 16, 22, 30, 35, 40, 45, 56, 65, 70, 71, 73, 78, 86, 87, 92, 93

Q

quadrant, 8

R

Renaissance, 6, 16–18, 23
Roman Catholic Church, 15
Roman Empire, 14
Rustichello, 20, 49

S

slaves, 64, 67, 83
Soderini, Piero, 49

T

Taprobana, 71
Theon, 10
Toscanelli, Paolo, 35, 78
Travels of Marco Polo, The, 20
Trinidad, 59, 60
Tropic Zone, 58
Tupi-Guarani, 79–86

V

Vespucci, Amerigo
    childhood of, 23–25, 26–28
    cultural observations of, 7, 79–86, 99
    education of, 29–30
    and financing of Columbus's second voyage, 38
    illness of, 67, 90
    letters by, 7, 41, 43–45, 48–52, 53, 73, 76, 82, 96, 97
    marriage of, 90
    and naming of America, 7, 41, 93–96
    personality/beliefs of, 6, 7, 22, 63, 99
    voyage for Portugal, 68–87
    voyage for Spain, 53–67, 68
    working for Medici family, 31–33

W

Waldseemüller, Martin, 92–93, 96

About the Author

Kurt Ray has written books on a variety of subjects for young adults.

Photo Credits

Cover © Scala/Art Resource, NY; p. 4 © Réunion des Musées Nationaux/Art Resource, NY; pp. 9, 59, 77 © Mary Evans Picture Library; pp. 12–13, 17, 19, 54, 57, 98 © North Wind Picture Archives; p. 21 © Art Resource, NY; pp. 24, 27 © Alinari/Art Resource, NY; p. 28 © Franz-Marc Frei/Corbis; pp. 32, 42 © Hulton/Archive/Getty Images; pp. 34, 37, 39, 46–47 © Giraudon/Art Resource, NY; pp. 50, 94–95 © General Research Division, The New York Public Library, Astor, Lenox and Tilden Foundations; p. 62 © Herzog August Bibliothek, Wolfenbuttel/A.K.G, Berlin/Superstock; p. 66 © Archivo Iconografico, S.A./Corbis; p. 69 © AFP/Corbis; p. 72 © The Huntington Library, Art Collections, and Botanical Gardens, San Marino, California/SuperStock; pp. 74–75, 84–85 © Corbis; pp. 80–81, 89 © Bettmann/Corbis.

Series Design and Layout

Tahara Hasan

Editor

Joann Jovinelly